The Book Collector

T0151875

Other Books by Tim Bowling

Low Water Slack (poetry, 1995)
Dying Scarlet (poetry, 1997)
Downriver Drift (novel, 2000)
The Thin Smoke of the Heart (poetry, 2000)
Darkness and Silence (poetry, 2001)
Where the Words Come From: Canadian Poets in Conversation (editor, 2002)
The Paperboy's Winter (novel, 2003)
The Witness Ghost (poetry, 2003)
The Memory Orchard (poetry, 2004)
Fathom (poetry, 2006)
The Bone Sharps (novel, 2007)
The Lost Coast: Salmon, Memory and the Death of Wild Culture (memoir, 2007)

The
BOOK
COLLECTOR

TIM BOWLING

NIGHTWOOD EDITIONS

2008

GIBSONS, BRITISH COLUMBIA

Nightwood Editions
P.O. Box 1779
Gibsons, BC V0N 1V0
Canada
www.nightwoodeditions.com

THE CANADA COUNCIL | LE CONSEIL DES ARTS
FOR THE ARTS | DU CANADA
SINCE 1957 | DEPUIS 1957

Cover design & typesetting
by Carleton Wilson

Cover photograph
by Milo Baumgartner

BRITISH
COLUMBIA
ARTS COUNCIL
Supported by the Province of British Columbia

Nightwood Editions acknowledges financial support from the Government of Canada through the Book Publishing Industry Development Program and the Canada Council for the Arts, and from the Province of British Columbia through the British Columbia Arts Council and the Book Publisher's Tax Credit.

Printed and bound in Canada

ACKNOWLEDGEMENTS:
Event, Fiddlehead, Malahat Review, Queen's Quarterly. "The Book Collector" won the *Fiddlehead*'s Ralph Gustafson Prize in 2007.

LIBRARY AND ARCHIVES CANADA CATALOGUING IN PUBLICATION

Bowling, Tim, 1964–

    The book collector and other poems / Tim Bowling.

ISBN 978-0-88971-235-5

    I. Title.

PS8553.O9044B67 2008   C811.54   C2008-905824-0

Contents

It Happens Now

It happens now.
As the businessman in the café declares
"It's a new world," blowing on his green tea
to display his globalism, it begins,
another salmon run to the Fraser River.
Several million sockeye hang at the mouth,
a swarm at the entrance to the hive,
turning their hunger inland, all feeding done,
surviving only on the fat they've stored
at sea; their hard flanks ripple,
their dark eyes bore into the planet's flesh,
their jaws gape, streaming silt and seaweed.

"People are sick and tired of the same advertising."

And all the wrecked cars in the marshes,
the orchards, the barnyards of failed farms,
turn with them, the hoods slowly lift,
the caskets in the parlours and the earth
adjust to the motion, people look away
from the sea, the east-facing windows fill
with bliss and despair, like pages
in poetry books from another century,
forgotten but still alive, keeping a little
pulse going in the dust and foxing
under the dim library lights
as the salmon throb in the chemical flow
and sewage, and hold their position, and wait.
The streets are still. Drivers have climbed

from their cars, store signs suddenly announce
We are closed but we are open.
please note our new hours,
the garter snakes in the bills of the herons
twist their almost-severed heads,
harbour seals surface darkly, water-bowed,
like pallbearers at an Irish funeral
glaring through hot tears at the coast of England
shouldering the wood no trees can grow,
clouds shudder above the massed schools,
yacht sails billow with the flow of horse blood
and piano music, a woman puts her bare foot
on the earth of a garden she planted
with her husband, now dead, whose bones
revolve as they settle. It happens again.
The past is the only dead thing that smells sweet.
Nothing is original, only authentic.
No longer to believe in Eden, but to be Eden.

The salmon return. Ghosts
with human skin and poets' eyes.
Death with one sting. Smoke
with the weight of sperm. Phantom pregnancy.

Metaphors for the absence of metaphor.
They return. Fish with fish skin
and fish eyes. At the first drop of rain
they will begin to die. Again.

In the future, the winners will be those who can't hive the wild swarm.

Triptych

1: *Against the Prophets of the Age*

She whistled me in from fields of play
with the song of the red-winged blackbird.
October, and her hands showed russet,
blood smeared her apron
and her brow. Yet her eyes, like ours,
were always more the preyed upon
than predator's. I came
across the twilight and the bluejoint grass
the fir-cone carpet and the street
of scales, with the real birdsong descending
to the one loved variant
on her lips, I'm coming for the kiss
that will be cold but isn't yet,
are you coming? I want you to come
before it's too late, I want you to meet
the virtues as they are in the flesh
and not the creeds, I want the blood
slick from the guts of the pheasant
and still slick on her cheek and mine,
on yours, the blood from the cut
in the sockeye's neck a poppy's mark
below the eye-socket bone, the blackbirds
singing into the encroaching dark
and a woman singing with them,
then, and now, though the grass
is gone, the fir trees down, the few
salmon clutching their coin

9

and shivering in their dwindling,
no pheasants in ditches or men
to bring them home, the dog's bark
and the moon's light
surgeoned at the chords,
but still the autumn lampshine
and a door to the warmth
and a voice you know
as well as your body; that isn't gone,
it's franced to your pallor
— inviolate transference of selves —
touch it, the wind cannot erase it,
you're hurrying in from the fields of play
to everything wonderful in the human spirit
and you will lie down in the greatest peace,
a child with a blood kiss, and wake
half a lifetime later
and look around, and feel the wound

fresh and dripping as the blackbird's song.

II: *Domestic*

My ten-year-old sister's hair is the Nass —
moonless nights, mythology, and rain-scent.
She sits cross-legged on the braided mat
amongst the boots and guns, and strokes
the crushed velvet of a mallard's throat.
Her tears are older than she is,
drops off a raised cedar paddle.
Her fingernails — tombs for the wild.

Her blood — a sunset for loon cry.
Her bottom lip — the spirit's windowsill.
Behind the blind she makes in the room,
I wait for truth to be flushed.

The dog whose jaws gently closed
on the limp bird's neck
pants outside the door;
he wears half the salt marsh in his coat,
he's a prince with an animal's breath,
he's waiting to push in
and pass the bloodied down on his tongue
to my sister's cheek.

An hour later
my father brushes my sister's hair
in the lamplight, stroke and stroke.
Her throat is bare, her neck stiff,
she loves him, she's smiling.
My mother sweeps up the tears
and drops them in the sink
without a sound or break.

The truth sees us all
and does not scare or veer.

III: *Windpipe*

The part I never liked, she says,
the part that most upset me,
was taking out the windpipe.
I closed my eyes and reached.
Sometimes it snapped in two.
It was always slippery.

She looks away. Her lips are old now
that bore the blackbird's song
to whistle me home. Her eyes
close, she's reaching for the source
of the music that we lived by once
and, silently, invisibly, touches
my throat.

If you dripped candle wax
on the feathers, though,
they pulled out easier, she says

and pushes back her chair
with a scrape, and limps
to the sink, and starts
to do the dishes
while the dark slides in
over the river
like flesh over a flute
that has no stops.

A Time of Inconsequent Change

A time of inconsequent change
in a forgotten town, though the salmon
remembered the taste of the river
and the sun did make the tallow
of the daffodil. A child there, a creature
more eyes than thought, one spring morning
packed several raindrops and a forehead kiss
into a schoolbag and did not attend
the world's curriculum. A salt marsh silence
greeted his name on the roll, he bowed
his head and entered the six cold churches
of a vanished week, one after the other, and then
the mildewed grief of a Lord's Day dropped
its Victorian yoke around his neck.

Between each of the abandoned houses
of the pioneers who pioneered the European sigh
and tear in a soil claimed from tides
the child gazed at puddles so long and dark
they might have been the mirrors to whom
those lives delivered their surfaces.
"Remember us," whispered their voices,
"Remember yourself." And the child
widened his eyes and entered Wednesday,
kicked the watery moonlight and mousebones
of Friday's garret bedroom, while the words of the dead
dogged him, a creature too early for memory,
until each heartbeat came as a stifled cry.

Outside, the morning's thin light trickled
down the drain of the beached whale's
blowhole. A Greek widow unwrapped
Homer's night from her wrinkled throat and,
in a park of sodden grass,
the travelling fair from Arkansas
put its roustabouts to work
setting up amusements for the living:
the rides, the games, the funhouse
with its loud, distorted surfaces.

The child's week that would be a man's
did not abate, nor did the red-winged
blackbird's shrapnel wounds forgive
the secrets of the cenotaph.

It was a man in a time of inconsequent change,
a forgotten man, a father in a child's frame,
who ascended the staircase of obsolete
worship to reach the rain-gnawed roof and sing,
who dragged the cracked mirrors of salmon
up the gangway of an uncherished place
and saw himself, and sees himself,
a thousand deceptions
on the condemned surfaces of life.

1972

Harvest was playing. Shirtless,
the shade of Roman breastplate bronze,
my brother mended sockeye net.
Early August. With his hair down
below his shoulders, he looked like Jesus
helping John. Through the open window
of his sea-green '69 Mustang fastback
Harvest was playing. Over the mudflats
drifted the chloroform of ripening corn.
My brother's quickness bruised the meshes.
He corrected the past with needle-flicks
and sipped a second or a third Labatts.
Incomparable catcher of the curviest pitch,
dater of twins, master of blue eyes, bluer depths,
who could at will affect a gallant flirt
with an aged Greek widow and then sneak
off behind the Arms or Drake for a toke
with jumpy Yankees
newly fled from Nixon's unctuous yoke,
he believed in but a single cause: the open heart.

We were the future together. The air
that would give the heron's skull its turn
to shine in the sun washed over us.
I was still young enough to be accounted for
by niches in the framework of the kitchen door.
And I loved without question a libertine Jesus
cast in Caesar's bronze who listened all summer
in days of uncut corn and nights oily

with salmon runs to a song
sung for an old man by a young
who urged him to take a look at their lives.

Near and far as the autumn moon
that would rise suddenly behind
one of the delta's star-crushed barns
a whale's back broke the surface calm.
Gulls screamed. Blood flecked the sun.
My brother's shoulder roiled
in the snag and wash of time.

Three decades on,
Harvest is playing. I hit repeat
on the sixth track, think of calling
across the provinces to where Rome
has fallen, is falling.
Instead, I sip at
a second or a third Labatts.

New day,
day, like all days,
fated for loss,
be more than an endless looping back,
be a young shoulder in the sun,
be heron-strike, the uncut corn,
be the heretical act,
be whaleback.

Our Lives Since Moving Away

Today the landlord asked if he could store
in our basement an old church pew
that's been rotting on his deck
("Your kids can play on it").
I fingered in my left pants pocket
the second tooth to fall out
of our firstborn's mouth,
said yes. The rain's steady.
My wife removes her makeup of tears
to reveal tears. I stay up late
with the grief in the cello, put off
writing Christmas cards.
Garbage collection's Tuesday.
The view takes your breath away
and you'll never get it back.
Nothing to breathe here
but woodsmoke anyway.
How are the kids? Better to ask
how are the stars: their abidance
astonishes when we remember
to notice. Like this heavy earth
we go on with our circuit
beneath fixed wilderness.

Molten pewter poured into casts
ceaselessly,
that's the sky and ocean
hissing around mountains.
And the difference between cloud and mist

is known only to the great blue herons
who wear airmail-coloured Canada Post uniforms
and take long smoke breaks
on the government wharf.
I'm afraid to ask them what they know.

Ah, but why not share the secret?
Sighs *do* have sequence:
loss, loss, and loss.
Each night washing dishes
I watch the widows walk their dogs
through drizzle into forest
and wonder at each leash —
surely need is sinew enough
to hold the little of life we've tamed.

We haven't even hung our paintings up!
They lean on the walls
like the teenaged friends
our teenaged kids will have.
I'm half afraid we'll wake in the morning
and find everyone gone,
watercolours, oils, flesh and blood,
and the house packed up, the movers
estimating the weight of the past
and suggesting kindly
we might want to leave it off the truck.

What do you want? I hear the universe ask.
I want what I can't keep from losing
I want to nail with a child's tooth
this painting of us missing you

and sit before it on a plank of faith
rescued from the rain
I want the holes not to be there
that have to be there,
the absence that, filled,
only widens.

How can nothing change, and everything?
Tides, mists, roads like whaleback,
and five people with five hearts
ghosting their way
from then to now
who could easily be five others
but remain who they are
speaking in hushed voices
in a spiderweb town
hanging from the points of love
between them.

Nothing. Everything.
Life has a way of just straining the leash.
That explains how a man,
in the midst of a dream of childhood,
suddenly wakes to strangeness,
struggles up, having aged
despite his dream,

to slip the coin beneath the pillow.

After Arrival

For months my mood was low.
I went out to stare through the prison bars
of the heron's stance, dragging the rain-sky's
blood-drenched nobleman's cloak.
Some life in the salt depths of me
tried to breathe out the skinned-over hollow
at the base of my throat. Each day
I felt it beach itself and die.
What was wrong?
Absence had been winched up on the ways.
Men in black oilskins scraped the invisible hull.
They wore the faces of men from my childood,
men I knew were dead, they whistled songs
found at the bottom of wooden radios.
I took the same walk past them every day
and never said hello. Beyond,
where the shoreline opens to the Sound,
the usual Baba Yaga bottle picker
rattling her green-slimed shopping cart
cackled "Bring out your dead!"
and winked as she knotted her scarf at her chin.
I chilled my hands at her medieval fire.
What was wrong? Skiffs overturned
and dragged up on gravel; I passed six,
eight, a dozen. Under what giant walnut shell
was I meant to find the sun?
I turned them all over.
Crabs of foul dark scuttled free.
Across the horizon, a tugboat pulled

a barge of oily feathers
and a barge of arid bones.
I was hanging in my life
like the wet rope
between flight and what's flown.

Can it be, in the end,
we change to accept change,
no yellow thrust of daffodil
without at first despair? The sun broke through.
The heron lifted. My friend, the kingfisher,
stout heart and blue coil,
agreed out of pity
to leave my salt in the sea.

GIBSONS MOMENT

This is a postcard of a sad expression in mist.
I'm trying not to think of it
as what we'd send from anywhere,
being so briefly alive, the heart a ghost
trying to break with a quick little fist
its trap of flesh. Today I started to cross
in mist the intersection at the paved crest
above the pebbled shore and seagulled wharf.
It's a town of light traffic. I left myself
only a second to pause, to hang my half-step
above this stretch of brine-and-cedar-scented earth,
my eyes for the moment full of the moment,
the steep grade down to shouldering tide and
heron's slouch, when suddenly it drifted up
from the diaphanous white — open-jawed shark! —
a pick-up grinding gears, its back
heaped with death, eight times death,
a bucket pulled from some slimy depth
by a grinning dark. I froze as it passed.
Eight carcasses bloody-pulped at the neck,
sandpapery slabs. Cargo of headless deer.
Haphazardly jumbled in, simply tossed
from the chainsaw or butcher blade
to catch like bone in this long throat of mist
and be hacked up. History's boxcar.
Cabin-floor of teenagers killed
in their sleeping bags. Back of my look,
the last look of life: serenity, fear,
the tongue tasting what it's born to,

eight quick blinks in breaking mist
behind my blink, the little wake
in the heave of my blood. Sad ghost,
what exit can your cobwebbed fist
make in the heaviest fact of us?
Exit that's not entrance
for the surge of black behind the dyke?

Then the gulls cried below me. I woke
to a present neither joy nor pain
and crossed the road and drifted home

along the edge that cut that bone.

Between Rainfalls

The crow is frenzied with his wings.
Shakespeare writing with both hands.

His call is an undertaker's sob
in the middle of the night
when he can't rub the powder
or the wax off his skin.

I look his eye in the eye.
I don't even blink when he pulls out my heart
and flaps up and drops it
on the rocks to effect a crack
to get at the meat.

It's a Tuesday morning in my forty-first year.
My year of crows and mist.
More crows and mist than a Scottish battlefield.
There's still a tag on my toe
from when the movers moved us
and all our worldly goods
across a border.
I think I'll keep it there.
I want to be sure to get where I'm going
when the only choice left is to go.

My heart? The crow's inspired.
This is his great soliloquy.
Again and again he flaps up.
Again and again I'm broken.

I laugh and laugh. 41 years, you bastard!
He can't understand where the sweetness is.

What Is Best for the Children?

Do you understand? I'm a father.
I wear the question as a stray wears a burr.
It lives in me as water in a wave.
It eats my boulder to a pebble.
If I see a grasshopper tangled in the spiderweb's hair
If a star's death-light laps the salt in the sea
If today it's decreed to paint the convent's brick
I have to know — is it best? Is it the very best?

It rained heavily in the night.
The manager of the bank steps over slugs
to reach his paper statue of decision
the crows run like mascara
the gulls are clean as sucked cherry pits
and no one can tell me. I phone my mother.
Five-feet-three-inches of love and loss.
Her eyes swim with the undeveloped negatives
of two dozen funerals, a dozen births.
I ask, and she says, "It is you,
the answer is you." I know she's lying.
What choice does she have?

Look. We're walking down a blue-veined road.
The bordering blackberry prickles
are snakes killed in battle with the Sioux.
Honeysuckle off the corpses. My children dance
in my shadow, fervent with the making
of the wine of my departure.

When they drink it, my father's dregs
stir in the cask,
a wasp circles the mouth of the gourd,
October sips the salmon's vintage.
Is it best?

Go away. No one can talk to me.
I'm a father and I lack an answer.
Do you understand? What do I care
if your knees have bled all over
the chalk figures on the sidewalk
your children left before they climbed
on the constellary rack
and disappeared into the forest?
The red dust of crab shells in your hands
the sinew of the cedar in your hands
a ladleful of ebb in each eye. Go away.
You have nothing to say.

This is the breadline for the corpse.
This is the hunger that grows with feeding.
This is the eclipse you have to watch
through the smoked flesh of the forearm.

Today in the downpour I take the clothes off the line,
my children's clothes, the sodden ghosts of the years,

and fold them and bury them away
in drawers sloshing sea water
in rooms where the whale's last breath
twirls the ballerina on the box

and the only music
is the longing of the cheek
for the aisle walk of the tear.

THE RETURN

I couldn't get out of bed this morning.
It isn't what you think,
not illness or a hangover. Simply,
I'd become a tributary of the Fraser River
and the last wild salmon
had chosen my body in which to dig her redd.

I lay with my blood furrowed
and my bruised flesh an autumn sky.
I could hear the eagles thinking far above
and the grizzlies' haunches snapping sinews as they ran
and the glaucous-winged gulls waiting to gorge
on the delicacy of a death-limned eye
which was revolving in me, deep,
seeking already a farther redd
to drop more eggs. But I was it,
her only stream. And she was
the only fish. No hook-snouted male
would fertilize the future with his milt.

I tried to roll over on my side.
The dull sun winked near each bank.

I lifted my hands.
Two leaves spun on the wind.

I shouted.
A star opened its mouth.

My wife and children stood around the bed.
Their shadows cooled the spawner's thrash.
I couldn't wipe their tears away.
My back was heavy, drenched with space
yet flowing, full of death, feeding
the descending world, I was more alive
than I'd ever been, but lost,
the last fungus-sided salmon clogging my throat,
my children seeking to unlock my eyes
with their tears, not seeing the roe
in the shallows of my leaving...
Cup your hands, I tried to say,
and save us. But they saw, as I saw once,
only a father dying,
and all I owned was what the wild gave me
at the end, my death in my own place
and the wake of glaciers to bear it to the sea.

The Human Condition

Why are the days not enough?
And the sky? Why is love
not enough? Here is a bush
I've never noticed,
purple-blossomed, white-
tipped, and here is a stranger
speaking Spanish to another
stranger — they're not enough.
Down the hill in the harbour
the speedboats' wakes
like blown dandelion seed
and no sound of the engines —
I'd never really noticed this,
but it's not enough.

Tomorrow, perhaps,
it will be glory again,
almost too much life
in a single tree
the sound a bird can make,
somewhere a blue whale
sliding its continent between continents,
or perhaps, still,
it won't be enough,
will never be enough,
the defeat will be permanent
without even the desire
to ask why,
why are the days not enough?

And the sky? Why is the blood
so thin that once ran freshet
and all the words clichés
and all the thoughts opinion

when the earth is here just the same
and the driftlogs change position
with each tide
and the blue scarf of the heron
is blown to the stars

why are the stars and our love not enough?

Four Postcards

Four postcards of famous paintings, the backs blank
as the Strait of Georgia in front of me. I think
I shall write to God, I think the cast
of His presence ought to be signed, at least.
Wishing you were here (sort of). Heal quick (or don't).
Van Gogh, Cezanne, Kobayashi and Klimt.

Twilight. The air breathes like the side of a doe
waiting to give birth. A fawn's come. Look!
There's a smudge on all that level pewter. Look closer.

It's a harbour seal
singular as a piano stool
on a stage long after
the concert's over
and the piano's
been rolled away.

On my lap
the hands and the white gloves
of the famous dead pianist.

A silence like a mother's silence
in the presence of her sick child.

The seal's note
melts into the sea.

That Laughing Casket, the Killer Whale

That laughing casket, the killer whale,
surfaced once beside my early years
and bore a life of heartbeats down.
Oh and its teeth flashed white as paper children
and they linked their arms around cloven satin.
The breath was all moonbroth and the blood of seals
and a vaporish girdle for the globe.
I stood in the draft from the open door
to the room of my conception
and the desuetude of middle age
dropped lightly on the bier.

Where does wonder go? Ask the owl
who splices the blowhole's spout
and wears the dew of grandeur
as it kills. Ask the little town
that breathes against the fog
that contains the mating cry of continents.
Ask the widow who sighs against her veil.
The days drip like candle wax
from a flickering flame in the eye of a boy.

His burn, our provenance.

PLAYING TALL TIMBERS

We drove an hour inland from the mouth of the river
to hit little white balls into little black holes.
He swam four years to die in a creek
splayed across the dogleg of the fourteenth fairway.
I found him when I bent to look for
an errant five-iron approach shot. Slime-green,
lobster-red, fungal, fraying his battle-flag,
he was a foot of salted barnacles
finding a desperate beach. "Dad,"
I called. But you didn't turn;
your hearing was getting worse. Next year
you'd need a cart, the year after...
we'd almost come to the end of games.
I fished briefly in the trickle
for what was mine, familiar by name,
while his lookless gape gaped on
through tatters. Unsuccessful,
I took my penalty and dropped.
On the green, in autumn's rust,
we joked, but were gentlemen,
as always, over our putts.

I can see us now, watching.
The balls turned slow as the planet
your weight would soon be leaving.

Father, my courteous maker,
in all the years that we killed them,

I saw no tears in the eyes of the salmon,
except the river, except the wide and searching waters of the world.

Names

I wanted to kiss Lianna Gould more
than I'd ever wanted to do anything
and so, walking along with Doug Shawn,
I lied and said my mom wanted me home
and then I cut down the lane between
the Daisy Dell and Vandermeers'
Butcher Shop, thinking of... of...
how she flicked her long blonde
hair out of her eyes as she stood,
gasping, one bare foot on top
of the soccer ball, and Danny Papuc
and Dave Chernenko and Brandon
Hughes all vanquished on the lawn
of windfall apples and horse chestnuts
gleaming and leathery beside their husks
and her saying nothing but meaning
"Come on, is that the best you can do?"

But as soon as I'd hurried out of the lane
to where Mr. Eustace was clipping
his immense laurel hedge and the Demostens'
brittle black lab leaned against his shadow
I saw Terry Godley (who always
ran the high school track as if
he had a broomstick shoved up
his bum, as Nigel Cash famously
said) and, worse, he saw me,
and I knew he was going
to ask if I had any spits

or gum or soaps and
he'd pay me back later. I didn't
even think about it – this
was the first time, as far
as I can recall, that I had
ever deliberately avoided
a social contact out of something
other than fear – I just ran
the opposite direction, past
Ivans the notary public's, not even
smiling at the image of Terry Godley
struggling along on his broomstick
behind me, his jaw razoring the air,
and in maybe five minutes
I was standing on the cracked
sidewalk in front of her collapsing
duplex where she lived crammed in
with two older sisters and four younger brothers
and, breathing hard, I waited,
as the salt breeze blew a couple
dozen leaves across my sight
for her to open the door and
walk out with the soccer ball
under one arm and her mouth
parted slightly to show the gap
between her front teeth – which
I always noticed before the spray
of freckles across the bridge
of her nose – and though I realize
it wasn't exactly twenty-three years
before that rain-eaten door
gave way and she stepped out

onto the recently-mopped and
glistening hospital floor where
my father and her mother lay
dying, it was as if we'd come down
from the almost-unbreathable air
of that first kiss and couldn't breathe
the common inrush of oxygen for minutes
as our eyes clicked over like odometers
and we had to begin the banalities
of courtesy and commiseration,
all the little clucks in the barnyard
meant to bolster the frailty
of the chicken-wire. And then, to learn
she had two children, one a girl
of almost ten, was not so much
a wound as a reminding caress —
remember how you lied
to Doug Shawn that time
just to see my bare feet
flicker over shadowed grass?

But we did not touch,
there between the last breaths
of our parents, though I thought,
perhaps, the simplest motion of
my hand towards her shoulder
might release the children
we had been, the horse chestnuts
glowing in the sundown light.
But release them for what?
The same future of putting
distance between us, the future

we share with almost everyone
or, more accurately to say,
everyone, the social act
of slipping away at last
the fundamental human act?

I thought of this today
for no reason that would satisfy
the rational age in which
we live, thought of it
as a boy thinks
for the first time
of kissing a girl
who stands
with her bare foot
on the round world
and all her blood at work
like a gasping fox
along the future's broken and unmendable fences.

THE SOCCER PLAYERS

Fifteen minutes into the first game of the season,
the first game of our lives,
he hadn't left the centre circle.
It was cold, the grass frosted, the lenses
of his glasses fogged. Our little mob,
all red cheeks and breath clouds,
roamed the field in a lost comet.
Not him. "Dooonaaald! Mooove!"
shouted our pig-snouted Scots expatriate coach
whenever our teams' two colours
whirled past like the death
of a limited autumn. He never did.
Except on rare occasions when
the rock-hard ball entered the circle.
Then, briefly forgetting his chewed-on sleeve,
he'd stab a chapped leg out and spin
the violating sphere away. And grin
to show his donkey's teeth. Who won
or lost mattered to a few fathers
every Saturday, the odd son. Donald's
parents never came. His sidelines
were so empty, he made his own
and drew them in.

Pathetic little Pythagoras of the heart!
Someone loved him enough, at least,
to strap the headband for his glasses on,
or did he do even that much for himself?

41

He was no one's friend and played
at no one's house. The whistle blew at the start and at the end
of every game, every season,
growing more shrill, until
we were older and he was
dead by his own hand. Well,

we all remember kids like that
or we forget them, the circles they made
to shut out the world, the sudden efforts
to belong when the world poured in.
I didn't care about his living statue
on the field, I didn't care when he died;
my lines were vague and always shifting.

Now they thicken, and there he stands
not even watching us, there he lies
colouring in his circle with his blood
to please a teacher who couldn't be pleased.

"Dooonaaald! Mooove!" The sky shouts.
The wind cries. The stars plead.
A father of boys, I cradle his head,
peer into the blurred lenses.
All around us runs the world,
that larger lens, the centre circle
of our lives, frosting over, autumn
dying, the colours coldly black
and white, blacker, whiter,
the sidelines empty. It's too late

but I position my body to cover
what can't be saved, and grin,

a second crosshair for the rifle sights.

Knicky Knicky Nine Doors

Hieroglyphed against the rainy dark
we knocked and knocked
on the doors of abandoned houses
trusting to trick even ghosts
the more delicious to fool
the more dangerous to anger.

A light comes on. Frayed branches
of the monkey-puzzle tree
reach out for their lost
Japanese gardener. Who's there?
Who is it? Hummocks of flesh
in the wet grass. It's us.
Yes, we love you this much,
though your cracked pool
is squalid with mulch
and rain and Halloween
brings no sugar to the tongue.

Neighbours, we hear you
on the stairs, the past
to a child is a velvet
bell-pull for service. Though
we ring for you, ghosts
of the town's first reeve
and lawyer, society wives,
yet still you come to us
bearing the silver salver
on which lies a message

that, read, will change
everything forever. Knock Knock.
Come out to us, neighbours,
we're coming in.

Somewhere a Child Is Growing Into His Magicianship

Somewhere a child is growing into his magicianship,
scarves, coins, cards, the rabbit of one word
pulled from the hat of another.
Somewhere the shrill end to the recess of the world
never comes and autumn leaves are not kicked
from the grave of the street of peremptory address.
Who held your hand when you walked off
into self? No one. Who holds it now?

Sun and moon, mother and father of no one,
bring your light to the rungs of this bone-ladder
where the assistant who is never us
closes the door to the cabinet and
knots the blindfold and whispers
down the years, "Ready?"

Somewhere a child does not turn from
the mermaid's lament for old form,
she changes a glass of sand
into a glass of water
and when she drinks
time does not fall through her.

Somewhere... we look back...
mother and father, an open hand,
what sleight of hand, what trick
empties every street
of the intimate enormity of shadow?

My Young Manhood Committed Suicide Last Night

My young manhood committed suicide last night.
I saw it fall as I approached the bridge
that spans Remorse and Regret. Had
the high beams on (it was foggy)
and saw the grass-stained shadow
and heard the silkworm's gnawing
at the unplotted affections
and felt an old woman's hand
on my forehead. Drove closer,
switched the cautions on,
clambered out. The white air
and the black, black sea
and no echo of the concussion
as if the wingbone of a gull
had struck the evening's velvet drum.
Bless your heart. There
but for the grace of God.
He who hesitates is lost.
The poetry was ancient and domestic,
direct as a letter in the hand
of a child writing to the future.
What was it saying?
What had it ever said?
When a piece of the self dies,
the ceremony must follow fast
upon the death.
I put on the black of the sea
and took the sharp edge of a star
to my shoulder and

47

unable to go forward or back
on that terrible bridge
rose like a flower
from the watery grave
and bore the associations of light
to the sun.

OUTSIDE OF THE WRITING PROGRAMS

Born into Calabrian poverty, shipped alone at nine to Halifax
and then by rail to Rupert's rain and
salmon mists. Dumbly, I asked,
Have you ever read perhaps Pavese?
Cesare Pavese? He blinked
as he must have blinked
half a century before
possessor of a peasant Italian, shivering
on the terrible precipice of English.
One blind eye embalmed in
diabetic smoke, the other a seal's brown
and spindrift. *No, no, I don't read,*
only write, always write. My wife,
she hates it, but what can I do?
Here, I show you. A binder black
as a grandmother's shawl, lugged up
from the seafloor of a life.
Two hundred and fifty poems. And every day more.
All five-foot two of him shrugs.
My kids, too young, what do they know?
My uncle used to say, you have kids,
you get wet, that's it. And smiles
in complicity.

I give him two years,
he's rotting from within,
his liver gone a decade since, his speech
reduced to slurs by strokes. He knows.
He wants to leave a record. At fifty-nine.

But what a record! Mankillers and she-devils,
lust and guilt and lust, the soul, the soul, the soul,
worship of a woman's flesh,
and love. All this
in single syllable end-rhyme
and more words spelled wrong than right.
Pavese! Diplomas in the drawer
must scorch and accolades
from critics shine like bile
in learned journals. What could I do?
What do you do every day of your life
with the slop of the world stuffed in at your eyes
all spittle and semi-blindness
and roving appetite for more, a son
and a daughter one table away, solicitous
for the natal blood that has endured
a child's wrenched affections, and endures
such loneliness as only death
stalking in his evil coat
can portion out? Nothing. Nothing.

Into common hands, the common binding.

On Two Lines by Edvard Munch

The sun set. I felt a tinge of melancholy.
Why not turn away from the man at the corner?
After all, it's the dead we talk with mostly.

I stayed up late, waiting for the rain to stop.
It never did. A dozen more moving boxes to empty.
My own hands committing my own surgery.

Parents! Siblings! Childhood friends!
Flesh is an inadequate packing for the heart.
Shadows lengthened over the half-empty boxes.
Why not look back? It's the dead we talk with mostly.

On that Oslo street, in a different art,
the sun set, I felt a tinge of melancholy.

The blazing housefronts told the fuller story.
The living rise at daybreak.

But it's the dead we talk with mostly.

AMSTERDAM

Today a bird fell dead at my feet,
a sparrow heartstopped by cold.
I was alone in the pink light
of winter dawn on shadowless snow.
It was half the size of my hand.
Its wings were out, its beak shut.
It had nothing to do with my life.
I was just another Dutchman
on a lazy Sunday in a museum
rapt before a wall of fruit and game.

The death briefly entered my heart
then left. I write the moment down.
For a Sunday far after my life.
The stare back is the art.

In Edmonton at a showing of *The Seven Samurai*. The theatre packed.
One vacant seat, in front of me, and, I swear, the tallest Japanese
man in western Canada takes it as the brushstroke characters slash
the screen. Cut to:

Sound of salmon striking a net, thunking in dewy cords to the
hold. My father's grizzled face in profile, smoke-shrouded in a
cinematic rain.

Halfway through the film, the eldest ronin, contemplative, says
(in summary) *youth's dreams go unrealized, you find your hair's grey, your par-
ents are gone and you're all alone.* I'm not alone, though my hair has
greyed and I can often taste on my tongue the ash of my fath-
er's cigarettes. That taste is what art means — serious joy, serious
sorrow, watching such a film not for the battle scenes but for the
vigil at the grave. Subtitles on a tombstone, who can read them?
White letters, white background. The laughter of my father as we
watched, on a tiny TV, late at night, a samurai moon the attacking
bandits. How much my father loved those who flout the code, and
those who, bound to carry it out, appreciate the renegade.

I flout, mild ghost, and carry out.

After the film, up on my bike, no helmet, in heavy dark, over the
bridge across the North Saskatchewan (tear it down behind me,
men — that will secure the northern gate), high speed, into the
even darker valley, no light at all, trees crowding the trail, I'm
hunger in the vein of the creature who watches me from cover.
Pedal harder. Trust to risk. The peasant with the spear who'll

knock me off my mount. Any second now. Kurosawa's failed sui-
cide in the enveloping black. Soundtrack of no sound. Your death
in slow motion. My hands clutching salmon like slippery entrails
to my chest. No commercial breaks. Downhill. House of sleeping
wife and children just off-screen. Faster now. Bared to the flesh
in the imaginary rain, seared to the will of the tilt of the earth,
mouth open, and where there should be a cry of lament, a close-
up of pain, drops washing mud off the naked corpse, comes the
exhilarant hai of the worker who, knowing the bitterness of life,
stands in the path of his own hurtling stone, on which is written,
boldly, his death-date

and asks the tall intruder to shift a little sideways in his seat.

The Book Collector

for Harry Elkins Widener (1885–1912)

I have less than twenty-seven minutes to write this poem
about Harry Elkins Widener who drowned
on the *Titanic* April 1912 with or without
his recently purchased second edition (1598)
of Bacon's *Essais* which, romantic accounts
insist, he leaped out of a lowering lifeboat
to retrieve, less than twenty-four minutes now
to tell you I've struck a seemingly benign iceberg
in my life and I'm hastily yet tenderly
ushering the consequential memories
into the ice-jagged sea and standing back
as the ropes creak and my father's
pipe smoke aspires with the hymns
to a heaven almost universally believed in,
eighteen minutes to acknowledge the death
of youth's purchase, seventeen minutes
to blink at my mother's diminishing shade
as the china slides and crashes
and the crushed velvet in the ballroom
loses forever the echo of the steps
of the past. An old man cries
composedly, and out of the dark
a woman shrieks words in the just-learned
tongue of terror, I am down to twelve minutes
and what am I going to say to you,
stowaways at the rail of another's heart,
that can bring you faster across
the killing waters? I must address

myself instead to the running-out sand
in the glass of Harry Elkins Widener
who did not live to spend the whole
of the family fortune on Shakespeare Folios
and Gutenberg Bibles but slipped into
the relentlessly clattering
press of tragedy and history
and became blank, void
as the sea and the sleepless hours
of the woman who bore him. Harry,
I have six minutes, and after them
I will live, I will walk in this body
on the earth as the iceberg
that will kill me bows and
retracts like a dancer from your era
to wait in the wings for ten
or twenty or forty years,
but tell me, what is the material
to what can only be, at essence,
spirit? Should I in my dwindling minutes
divest myself of the armature
of belief in printed expression to succor
and sustain? Three minutes. Two.

Young Mr. Widener, Sir,
you didn't go back for the book,
you didn't even think of it
or of Shakespeare or Gutenberg
as the ship tilted like a parched throat
beneath a cracked glass. Romance
is a luxury of the living and you
were several staircases down on your way to death,

and we who have made a start behind you,
gathering and spending, turning the rare pages
with delight, shelving and reshelving
the accumulated wisdom
of the world, adherents
to the faith in permanence,
sniff the Alexandrian smoke
and turn over in our first-class berths
and steerage bunks or play
another hand of poker
as the lights flicker
and at last go out.

This is the final moment
of the final poem of my youth
which will be printed and bound
between covers and found perhaps
by others as I found your name, Harry,
by the serendipity of our common passion
for the rescue ship to arrive in time
and the tragedy to be told as comedy
by firelight some far-off year.

Goodbye, Harry. Goodbye who you were,
who I was, who we all were.
Peace to your unrecovered bones,
the hours lived.
Peace to the eternal ligatures.

SELF-PORTRAIT EXECUTED SWIFTLY

He thought in centuries and lived for the day
vanity like a madman chained in his breast.
Complexion of lard, eyes of black lacquer —
over a book, he always brought to mind
the Chinese saying: *Three days
without study and life loses its savour.*

I used to catch a glimpse of him
from time to time, in puddles,
glassed liquids, the bathroom mirror.
Whether the past or the present
killed him in the end, no one can say.

I suspect it was, as always and forever,
those barbarians massing at the gates.

There isn't time to write more. Excuse me,
Ramon Fernandez, you cannot possibly know

how quietly my understudy waits.

I step in to rid myself of myth.
Here are the rare books of the famous dead.
I take their cold hands; there's still a pulse.
Someone is wearing white gloves for a tome.
Glenn Gould at the keyless piano of time.
My little cough's a cough in a catacomb.

I move like a pen scribbling in a margin.
Can I see, please, the first-edition *North of Boston*?
The author's annotated *East of Eden*?
If my eyes drop south and I lean to the west?
The pianist eyes my noteless page,
silently strikes a chord of rage.
"Life isn't a tea break at a cricket test!"
I want to shout, but shouting's not allowed.
The only other sound's the sound of downy flake...
(but that's not right, and it's somewhere else).

In my pocket, hot as a copulating mantis,
the jackknife that I carry for a private lark.
They dim the lights when they want us out.
It's like standing on the *Titanic*'s deck.
Quick! The autographed copy of Hardy's verse!
Women and children and bookworms first!
Wait! You got any expensive Americana pre-Antietam?
That's right – I want to fondle your antebellum vellum.

In my jean jacket and Beatles mop, I stifle a laugh.
Inside every Alexander's a pig-eyed visigoth.
None of this happens, or it happens, or, worse,
it's only something inked between covers.

Because no one cares, I have to care myself.
The way I can recite all the names
of Edna St. Vincent Millay's lovers!

All right. That's more than enough.
I go out exactly the way I came
with my hands behind my back
in onion-skin cuffs.

My Wife Is Reading *Wuthering Heights*...

for the first time since she was twenty-four
and "It isn't the same." She smiles
and I know it's at her younger self
and not the book. "Heathcliff
is always gnashing his teeth. Back then
I thought that was true love." Smile,
rueful head-shake, an almost-blush.

Now my loneliness decides to laugh.

How unlikely love is, storm-crossed
or crossing moors, my wife in snowy Montreal,
sobering up, going back to school and books,
page after page, coffee in an endless cup,
not knowing how lovely she is, lips parted
as Heathcliff rages and breaks another crop
against the horse's flesh,
and me, alone in the stern of a salmon boat,
in rain, under sun, stars, so afraid of life
the salmon's was the only life I knew
by touch, and they were always dying.
My wife among the bricks and ice,
my self among the wood and brine:
somehow our bodies found the stream.

Now I look at her across the years
across the voices of our children
across the perfect ache of youth:
it's raining, but the moon is out,

full, drawing tides and blood,
bathing the faces of unwanted solitude,
clouds and horses darkly moving
to some assignation
where longing will be broken
forever, the manse boarded up, the wind
busy carving epitaphs out of the earth.

Count us blessed, but half-blessed only
who leave the early passion of the page
for life: something is lost, something
tender is always slipping away from us,
the love I couldn't give her then
the love I didn't give today

the different form our love must take

when all the words in all the books
are burnt grass on a snowy grave.

The Classics

Lying in bed with my daughter
after an after-midnight summer walk
and she still manic with the dark
and somehow the subject
of giants comes up (I think
we spoke of favourite fairy tales
and I mentioned the beanstalk
climbed by Jack). Sadie says
"I like the one where that man —
I forget his name — did the trick
with the sheep, remember?"

"Oh yes, you mean Ulysses
when he escaped from the Cyclops?
And he tied his men with ropes
underneath the sheep?"

"Yes."

Then on from there I told
my child who will become
a woman whose face
will doubtless launch a few ships
of its own in time
about the Trojan horse's
tragic, manoeuvring cleverness,
and while she considers this,
lying completely still on her back,
I think of the few years

my retired fisherman father tended a flock
of sheep for a farmer on a tiny island
in the Fraser River — winters,
and his breath and theirs
hung in a purer fleece, white
as the small full moon,
the blinded eye of Polyphemus,
how nimbly he moved among them
in their pen, with what gentleness
approached their needs. I see him
again for a rare moment
in the bedroom's fire-charcoaled dark
as if there'd never been a rope
around his spirit and a last escape
to the final stages of a journey
none of us could share. Finally,
Sadie says she'd like a Trojan horse in our yard
so she could hide in its wooden belly
and have a place where no one
could find her. And I do not reply
about the immense night
to which she's fastened already
by thought and touch, love, pain,
but instead reach out and stroke
her hair, the fraying strands
of the unintended trick
that leaves a father
staring wildly
into the sea-wrack
sobbing against the cliff.

September Grass

Too young for so much memory
I try to be the Trojan horse
in the camp of my own life,
a dangerous gift, all future
ready to transmute to myth.
But I lack the energy for an enemy.
If there was a dark wood left
anywhere in my country,
I'd come to it. Instead,
I walk past the clearcuts
and lie down and wake
by a window opening
onto September grass.

The mulch of crabapple windfall's
in my lungs, and in my eyes
the salmon's silver on the blades,
the wet that keeps the fish alive.
I didn't hear them in the night.
I didn't know I'd set the net again.
Slowly the sun burns off the film
and leaves the yard a cracked green skin.
Can we see anything for what it really is
if we don't wear our bruises
the way a tiger wears its bars?

Another apple falls and blackens out
an exit for its flesh.

I can't bear even the one terrible hairshirt
of change in the September grass.

The bathroom tap-water slips through my hands,
the film of each day's life and death.

November 1st

Empty the treat bag. The dark confection
is my origin. A gentleman of lean purse
I hire nonetheless
a car to cruise the river road,
this hem of a gypsy's skirt
out of which tumbles a town
whose faces and houses
look back the moon
with the burnt-black eyeholes
of the day after the night
of haunting. Who isn't haunted?
No DeMille can bear the close-up
of the tree in leaf, unleaved.
On the free endpaper of her books
Greta Garbo wrote, *Read
by Greta Garbo and Dog.*
The Roman candles cry
the darkness down.
I tell my man to drive.
The hunting owl's face is bone.
He slides along
the same parallel
abacus of terror.

Sugar fills the cavity.

Blankly, the dog's eyes
roam the page.

The Funeral of Tenderness

I myself walked at the funeral of tenderness
—John Berryman

I was the first to arrive
or the only to attend
until the jackrabbit
camouflaged between
snowdrift and snowfall
paid his respects
with the dawn light in his eyes.

All around us flowed the hymn
of pupae rending the veil
of green searching space
for the one blade of grass.
As we approached the casket
of bird-bone and beeswax
the breeze handed us
the starlight's brittle papyrus
which crumbled in our hands.

Though, as mourners,
we did not know each other,
it seemed we did, and had forever:
love for the dead
affixes all strangeness.
Our shy glances
were attempts to see the past
in which our friend had lived
with so much abandon

that a child's eye and a risen moon
were indivisible, the hair
on the world's wrist
could not hide its pulse.

Outside (and everything was outside)
a truck horn blared, a girl
in a schoolyard sighed,
a young man crossed against
the lights of his spirit
and a young woman's
hardened as it broke.
No one intoned *Dearly Beloved*
or *Ashes to Ashes*.
The tears shed
belonged to time
and time wasn't here.
Yet I could feel absence and presence
growing old together
a married couple
from long before the age of sepia.

Something owned the air
that did not value it
something stroked the rabbit's fur
that did not cherish it
something touched my mouth
that did not honour it.

The hand on the heart-side of my body
was empty
the hand opposite the heart-side of my body

was empty
my bones were in the rabbit
and they were in the corpse
and then the rabbit's bones
and the corpse's bones
were in my skin
the exchange was painless
and fatal to what was.

So ended the brief service
I attended by the chance only
of attention
and a fondness
for silence. If you were there
it is only right
I did not see you.
What has gone cannot be grieved
in the mass. First
comes recognition
of the hole in life
and then the process
of filling in
as dawn fills in
the eyes of those
for whom light is blood.

The rabbit started the clock again.

I had nowhere to go
except to follow
and nothing to say

returned at once
to the palpitations of being
and the sea.

The Childhood Wall

A child climbs the childhood wall
unscrews the glass eyes from
the mounted pheasants and mallards
and plays a game on kitchen tiles
over which a mother's shadow
seeps like a tide. The stakes
are the rest of his life. For now,
he's winning. His wild eye gazes
through the manufacture of the world
and sees another world — a man
at a desk who's trying to rise
above the burnishments
of hunted autumns. The man
wants to see death as it is
to a child — remote, intimate,
the firelight in the glass eye
of the flocks a vitality
from the heart of flight.
Child's play. Man's work.
The bird the gun is always raised at.
Among the approximating instruments —
open season on the real.

Riding a Bike at Sunset

Hello boyhood shadow.
How unlonely you are
in the consummation
of each moment
as you keep ahead
of the sweating present
and drained limbs of the past
how you race like a fish
from the tipped rod and cast
of an angler who hardly sees you
for the hunting of those depths
he believes you sounded
with every footfall along
the blackberry and honeysuckle-
hung path trod by the dead
and the insignificant living —
mice, spiders, children
whose each breath played
a piano key in a recital
juried by a row
of faceless clocks.

The wheels turn. Heavy-headed,
the sunflowers bow
to you, last liege of wonder
raimented in adornless black,
as you pass and the sun's
cut mouth sinks
into your nape. I follow,

hunched over the bars,
exultant, to assess
the moment's music
and award a mother's kiss
to the always-venturesome, rapt,
descending-in-last-light timepiece
of summer on the human face.

I Could Never Stay Awake

I could never stay awake
those year-long, river-swollen nights
of explosive blood and silver
with a Chinese poet's silence
strung between the mountain peaks
beyond Vancouver
and an empty rowboat
tied to Wilkies wharf
with a rope of old rain.
The exhaust fumes, the too-fresh
memory of the time
before time, compost
of the salmon's dying
and the child's forming
consciousness. My eyes closed
on the dark
and opened on the light —
it was that way for years of summers:
a man stood patiently against
all that I didn't understand
and sometimes, very softly,
he spoke my name.
But it was always too late,
I was already gone.

And then the hours came
when the man lay in a bed
in a room rank with antiseptic
and I could not fall asleep

though I was more frightened
than I had ever been
and had a greater need
of his strength,
hours of artificial light
the old dark tides
lapped against.
My eyes remained open
until his eyes
were done
with opening and closing.

Now when I softly speak his name -
nights I can't sleep
days I can't believe —
it's already too late
he's always just gone.

Winter Walk

Woodsmoke from chimneys
dogs' breath from doghouses
whalespout mist
for five seconds in the dark
and gone. The bees' brief truce
in their long Tet of work.

I hunt their summerlong lines
in the air above a man-made dyke
unmake two decades of my own.
As if you can find in the night sky
a moon never walked on, a moon
from a grandmother's girlhood
(no birth stains or bridal gown)
as if — at last — the simile
is the thing itself.

I used to fish in these waters.
Boy and man. Touched the gills
of salmon, those opening flowers
closed now, honey ungathered.
I used to be, like all of us,
someone else. The vessel of the past
can find no wharf but drift
and the bees' lost lines drag
from stern and gunwales. Turning,
I recover the living in their houses,
a fleet of fire-made masts

the tears of German children
on the ashes of the Jews.

Pheasants Slick in Ditches

Pheasants slick in ditches. Afterbirth of autumn.
Rain that falls with singular intent — to darken dusk as it settles
on constructed absence — of tombs, skiffs, bereft looks.
When a man begins to fill with memory
as a ditch fills with water, as a salmon's incursions
tend to rust, when the black scarecrow at the side
scares only the hand that casts the seed,
what is born is hard born,
words decline from the owl's clutch,
a honeybee hunts the surface of the moon.

What is the day? The face on a head pulled gasping
from the river and held tightly by the hair.
It looks and looks but cannot see, sheer
survival, the watch silent in the gill of the pocket.

Not an abstract man, nor any wet day of the world,
but this man, these years, this soaked field.
The muskrat going home — pool cue, ball and
velvet stroke — all life's letters
in their pigeonholes and no one to read them.
I touch the damp red stamp of the ditch.

It rises.

The day is the address of the sun.

About the Author

TIM BOWLING has published seven poetry collections and three novels. His first book of non-fiction, *The Lost Coast: Salmon, Memory and the Death of Wild Culture* (Nightwood Editions), was shortlisted for the Writers' Trust Nereus Non-Fiction Award and the Roderick Haig-Brown BC Book Prize, and won the Alberta Literary Awards' Wilfred Eggleston Award for Non-Fiction. *The Lost Coast* was also chosen as a 2008 Kiriyama Prize Notable Book. That same year, Bowling was the lone Canadian artist chosen to receive a prestigious fellowship from the John Simon Guggenheim Memorial Foundation. A native of the West Coast, he now lives in Edmonton.